Original title:
Thorny Thoughts

Copyright © 2025 Creative Arts Management OÜ
All rights reserved.

Author: Penelope Hawthorne
ISBN HARDBACK: 978-1-80566-610-3
ISBN PAPERBACK: 978-1-80566-895-4

Stabs of Insight

In the garden of my mind, oh what a scene,
Ideas poke like cactus, sharp but keen.
I wrestle with thoughts, a comical plight,
As I trip on wisdom dressed in daylight.

But laughter erupts as I dodge each jab,
Each prickly epiphany a mischievous grab.
Like a clown with balloons, floating so free,
My stabs of insight can tickle with glee.

Bramble Dreams

In a tangle of dreams, where laughter grows,
I navigate pathways with countless throws.
Each twist and each turn, a giggle ensues,
As I tumble through chaos with silly shoes.

Bramble my thoughts, oh what a delight,
I dance with the vines under the moonlight.
In a garden of whimsy, I safely scheme,
And wake with a chuckle from bramble dreams.

Sharp Edges of Silence

In hushed moments, sharp thoughts come alive,
Like a sneaky hedgehog, I try to survive.
With silence so thick, it can prickle my skin,
I laugh at my shadows, let the fun begin.

Each silent edge teases, a poke and a jibe,
Whispering secrets that tickle my vibe.
With humor in silence, I skip and I weave,
In a world full of giggles, I dare to believe.

Vexing Vines

Vines twist around thoughts, a puzzle to solve,
With every small tug, my laughter evolves.
They tangle my mind with a chuckle so wide,
As I wrestle with notions that bump and collide.

Oh, vexing vines, you bring such a game,
With tangled ideas that tease and inflame.
In the thicket of chuckles, I find my release,
As I dance with the chaos, my mind finds its peace.

The Sharpness of Silence.

In a room where no one speaks,
The clock ticks loud, a prankster sneaks,
A loud thought screams, but no one hears,
Just giggles trapped in silent gears.

A sneeze could break this quiet game,
Yet here we sit, all still the same,
Whispers dance like a playful breeze,
As awkward glances bring us to knees.

In this hush, the minds take flight,
Wit spins tales in the dead of night,
But with each grin, we seal our fate,
For laughter's short, mustn't be late!

So raise a cup to the noise of thought,
In silence funny jests are brought,
The sharpness here is quite a thrill,
As laughter hangs upon the quill.

Briar Whispers

In gardens where the roses bide,
I tickle thorns with silly pride,
A prickly dance on fragrant ground,
Where whispers of blooms can be found.

The bees dodge barbs in their sweet quest,
While I trip over nature's jest,
One little stumble, a yelp, a twist,
And there I am in flora's tryst!

Giggles float on the air so light,
As petals tease the bugs that fight,
With every poke, a chuckle shared,
In this wild patch, I'm never scared.

Briar whispers float on the breeze,
With joyful jabs that tease and please,
Among the thorns, I find my glee,
In nature's riddle, quirks roam free!

Jagged Reflections

In a lake where my thoughts collide,
Peering in, I cannot hide,
Each ripple shows a comical face,
Making fun of my own space.

A splash distorts the image bright,
Like laughter bursting in the night,
Reflections grin with wise old tales,
Of mishaps wrapped in joyful gales.

I see my brows in silly knots,
Debates with fish lead to funny thoughts,
With every glance, my worries fade,
As nature laughs at the fool I've made.

But swimming deeper is quite the jest,
Where mirth reflects on a world at rest,
Amidst the jagged joys I find,
Life's absurdities unwind, unwind!

Barbs of Dilemma

Caught between a laugh and sigh,
The choice is clear, though reasons lie,
A thorn in jest, a jest in pain,
Twist of fate, my thoughts refrain.

To poke the bear or let it sleep?
A question that makes reason leap,
Life's conundrums play the fool,
With barbed humor as my tool.

Each dilemma wrapped in wit's embrace,
Drawing smiles where troubles chase,
A prickly path where giggles spark,
Bringing sunshine to shadows dark.

So here I stand, with heart on sleeve,
In laughter's web, I choose believe,
That barbs of life, though sharp and keen,
Can tickle us to laugh unseen.

The Unfriendly Garden

In the garden where the weeds grow tall,
The daisies whisper, 'We're having a ball!'
But there lurks a gnome with a frown on his face,
He scares off the butterflies—oh, what a disgrace!

The roses are grumpy, they wrinkle their leaves,
While the tulips conspire and plot in their sleeves.
Every time the sun shines, the carrots complain,
"Why must we grow with this constant disdain?"

The sunflowers giggle, 'Just look at that berry,'
It wobbles and giggles, refusing to merry.
But every time laughter starts echoing near,
The turnips all shush—"Now, we mustn't appear!"

In the end, who's the culprit, that thorn in the side?
It's the pesky old cat who thinks he's a guide!
He prowls through the flowers, a ruckus he brings,
In the unfriendly garden—oh, what mischief he slings!

A Rub of Reality

I tried to scratch my back, oh what a feat,
With a branch from the garden—a thorny retreat!
It poked and it prodded, oh, what a surprise,
I thought I was clever, but I just made it rise!

My neighbor said, 'Grab this magic old stick!'
But that 'easy solution' just made things more thick.
I tripped and I stumbled, bumped heads with the fence,
Reality chuckled, 'Your logic's so dense!'

I swayed with the flow, trying hard to impress,
But the branches all whispered, 'You know you're a mess!'

A rub of reality? More like a scratch!
The garden's laughing—oh, who flipped the latch?

So here's to the thorns, the giggles they bring,
Through scratches and pokes, we still feel like kings.
In the rub of reality, it's all just a jest,
So I giggle and chuckle, and forget the rest!

Wrapped in Brambles

Wrapped up in the brambles, I found my way home,
Thought I'd take a shortcut, but met frosty foam!
The walrus beside me just chuckled, 'Oh dear!'
He wore a top hat and a grin ear to ear.

With legs all entangled, I danced with a tree,
It swung and it laughed, 'Come, join in with me!'
But the thorns were relentless, like tickles from fate,
I rolled and I tumbled—oh, how I can't wait!

A merry band of critters began to parade,
The hedgehogs were laughing, flaunting their spade.
With a twist and a turn, I spun like a top,
But the brambles just pulled me—'You're stuck here, stop!'

In this funny adventure, I learned something grand,
Though wrapped in these thistles, I still understand.
Life's whims are a puzzle, a riddle so bright,
In brambles, I found quite the laugh of delight!

Fractured Serenity

While seeking some peace, I climbed up the hill,
Only to trip on a patch of goodwill!
The daisies were dancing, they elbowed each other,
In fractured serenity, they laughed, oh brother!

A squirrel with a nut winked, 'Aren't we a sight?'
As I tumbled and stumbled, he offered delight.
'Life's filled with surprises, so join in the fun!'
But I stood there still, like a deer on the run.

A cardinal chirped, 'Hey, don't take it so hard!'
While I grappled with laughter, down by the yard.
With each clumsy twist and an awkward flair,
I joined in their ruckus, my worries laid bare!

In fractured serenity, my worries grew small,
Life's quirks remind me, I'm welcome to fall.
Through laughter and tumbles, I finally see,
That fractured moments can set our hearts free!

Splinters of Insight

In a garden where the weeds have grown,
I sat down on a very pointy stone.
My mind, a puzzled jigsaw spread,
Filled with thoughts that won't be fed.

Every poke brings a giggle and a sigh,
As I ponder why the bees all fly.
The flowers laugh, they know the score,
While I ponder pairs, like socks and more.

But wisdom blooms in odd locations,
Like finding art in faint vibrations.
So I tiptoe through this comical mess,
With splinters that teach in their own caress.

Prickled Echoes of Memory

Oh, the memories, they prance and play,
Like hedgehogs having their own ballet.
Each prick evokes an old, funny tale,
Of shoes lost in a garden, without fail.

Once I danced with a cactus near,
Thinking it held secrets, oh so dear.
But all I got were scratches and wheezes,
From a plant that just stabs while it pleases.

Yet laughter rings in the thorns we find,
Nostalgic tickles, oh so unkind.
Each poke a reminder, each twinge a grin,
These prickled echoes pull me right in.

The Cactus Heart

Once met a cactus with a heart of gold,
Its spines were stories, dangerously bold.
It whispered secrets I could barely hear,
Wrapped in humor, yet full of fear.

I reached out gently, trying to poke,
And found I'm the punchline of this joke!
With each little jab, I learned to behold,
That silly heart can be quite uncontrolled.

So here's to the laughter that springs from the pain,
Growing friendships in sunshine or rain.
For in every poke, there's a tickle to start,
A reminder that love often plays its part.

Jammed Between the Needles

Like a hedgehog stuck in an old sweater,
My thoughts get tangled, a jumbled fetter.
Lost threads and needles, all in a fray,
Wishing for clarity, come what may.

Some days I find my mind's on a stroll,
Chasing a thought like it's on a roll.
But the needles jab, and the laughter flies,
As I chuckle over my confused replies.

In jamming and poking, I see the delight,
In the mess of it all, the future's bright.
So here's to the tangled, the pricks, and the laughs,
For in all the chaos, joy often drafts.

Prickles of Reflection

In the garden of my mind, so bright,
Ideas poke and prod, a curious sight.
With every chuckle, a giggle may sprout,
Who knew deep thoughts could be such a rout?

Bumbling through thoughts like bees on a chase,
They buzz and they ricochet, wild in their pace.
Laughter blossoms, it's truly absurd,
As I tickle my brain with a witty word.

A cactus of thoughts, growing taller each day,
Pricking my sides in a humorous way.
My mind's a bouquet, a comical stew,
Who knew introspection would bring such a view?

So I stroll through this patch of fanciful fun,
Where prickly ideas dance under the sun.
With a grin on my face and a pun to apply,
I gather my jests and let out a sigh.

Vines of Contemplation

Twining around my mind, thoughts intertwine,
With leafy dilemmas dressed up so fine.
They tangle and tumble in jungles of jest,
Who knew pondering could be such a quest?

A vine creeping forth, it tickles my brain,
As I ponder the wonders of ketchup on grain.
In the tangled recess, a chuckle ensues,
What if socks talked—could they sing the blues?

I scale up my thoughts for a succulent view,
Each twist in my mind brings a giggle or two.
Contemplations with laughter, what a fancy affair,
Swinging on vines, without a single care.

With each little ponder that sprouts like a vine,
Humor's a flower, it's simply divine.
Through laughter I travel, a whimsical ride,
In this jungle of musings, I take it in stride.

Barbed Whispers of the Mind

Whispers dart in and out, pokey and sly,
Thoughts jab and they tickle, oh me, oh my!
In the corners of reason, hilarity stings,
With every sharp jest, laughter takes wing.

Encounters with barbs, they giggle and tease,
As I ponder if ice cream can dance in the breeze.
With each sharpened notion, they poke at the seams,
Creating a tapestry woven with dreams.

A jab here, a poke there, then suddenly—boom!
My logic erupts into giggly balloons.
Each barbed contemplation becomes a delight,
In the echoing chambers that rumble at night.

So here in my noggin, these whispers do play,
Spiking my joy in a curious way.
With humor as armor, I'm ready to glide,
Through the prickly thoughts, I take it in stride.

Twisted Pathways of Reflection

Down twisted pathways where silliness flows,
Reflections on life where absurdity grows.
I trip on a thought, then I giggle and twirl,
With each turn I take, I'm lost in this swirl.

A path made of giggles, lined up like trees,
Carrying whims like a gentle summer breeze.
The more that I wander, the funnier it seems,
Comparing my worries to runaway dreams.

Each twist brings a chuckle, a smile, or two,
What if my shoes decided to brew?
I stumble and rumble through humorous bends,
Waltzing with ponderings, laughter transcends.

These pathways of mirth, a delightful escape,
Where all of my thoughts wear a silly shape.
I'll stroll along gently, no hurry, just cheer,
In reflections so bright, I've nothing to fear.

Abstract Agonies

I tripped on my mind's wild vine,
Thoughts wrapped tight—a strange design.
They poke and prod, they twist and shout,
Giggling at the chaos sprout.

My dreams grow wild, they swirl and twirl,
Bouncing like a playful girl.
In one corner, I see a frog,
Dancing in a mental fog.

An idea jumps, then hits the wall,
It laughs and says, "You can't have it all!"
With each new twist, I try to grin,
Logging miles of nonsense kin.

Yet through the thorns of laughter's play,
I find a joy in disarray.
For every dark and jagged thought,
Brings a chuckle, freshly caught.

Enter the Bramble

Here come the prickles, one by one,
Dancing about, oh what fun!
A jig of jumbled ideas, bright,
Spinning 'round with sheer delight.

What's that sneaking? A rogue balloon!
Floating high, singing a tune.
It pops at once, oh how it stings,
But laughter's echo swiftly rings.

I walk through thickets, skip and hop,
Dodging thoughts that want to stop.
Each tumble leads to fits of glee,
Because chaos always sets me free.

So here I bounce, a carefree sprite,
Amid these brambles, oh what a sight!
With every poke that tickles me,
I laugh aloud, just let it be.

Thorny Soliloquy

Inside my head, a broad parade,
A lively show where thoughts are made.
They pirouette through bramble's grasp,
With jests so witty, I nearly gasp.

One jester squeaks, a mouse on skates,
While another juggles odd-shaped plates.
Each tumble generates a laugh,
In this absurd little math.

But lo! A thought can take a stab,
Like poky thorns in a bad cab.
Yet with each jab, I flip and twirl,
Finding joy in this goofy swirl.

So let them poke, let them tease,
I'll pen my woes, I'll laugh with ease.
For in this wild, chaotic show,
I find the fun, let thorns just grow.

Irregular Petals

In a garden full of quirky things,
Petals flutter, like paper rings.
Each color's odd, a sight to see,
In a bloom uncouth, just like me.

A dandelion wears a crown of style,
Winking at the weeds with a smile.
"Oh, poke me not," the rose does plead,
While the daisy giggles, "I'm free indeed!"

With every poke, a chuckle bursts,
From hesitant buds that quench their thirst.
One babbling brook talks 'bout the thrill,
Of petal pranks and impossible spills.

These irregular blooms dance in the breeze,
With thoughts that tickle and always tease.
Life's a garden of laughter's blooms,
Chasing away the pointed glooms.

Wounded Blossoms

In a garden where giggles dance,
Petals pout like they've missed a chance.
I asked a rose for a piece of advice,
It said, 'Avoid the bees, they're not very nice.'

The daisies are trapped in a ping-pong game,
While violets grumble, 'We're never to blame!'
Tulips argue about who stands out,
Yet all of them yell, 'What's that buzz all about?'

Laughter hangs thick like dew in the air,
As thistles try their best to wear flair.
They dress in sequins, but they're oh-so-tacky,
While dandelions float, getting a bit hacky.

In this hilariously prickled land,
Even the cacti can't quite make a stand.
With jokes that sting and colors that pop,
These wounded blooms teach us joy never stops.

Gnarled Pathways

On the path where the weeds tell jokes,
I met a snail, who wore fancy cloaks.
He said, 'Watch out, my friend, for the mud,
It's a comedy show turned into a dud!'

Branches twist like they're doing ballet,
While squirrels debate the best nuts for the day.
The sun is tickled, it can't stop its beams,
Lighting up mischief and nature's wild schemes.

Roots try to dance but often trip out,
With flowers laughing, they're forget-me-nots stout.
"Let's plant some humor," chirp the old oaks,
And share a few giggles with all silly folks.

Each step you take leads to some playful shove,
Where laughter's the treasure that gardens dream of.
In gnarled pathways, life's silly, it's true,
With jokes about thorns and an occasional boo!

Discomfort's Garden

In a patch where discomfort creeps near,
Plants overact, oh my dear!
A cactus complained, 'I need a new pot,'
While daisies tossed petals like they were caught.

The thorns threw a tantrum, all in a huff,
Complaining that friendship is really quite tough.
'Why can't we whistle like the birds up high?'
But their pricked little fingers had to comply.

Roses snickered, 'We don't want to prance,
Let's just throw a ridiculous dance!'
And so they jived, with roots on the floor,
Causing a ruckus, oh, what a lore!

Comfort is lovely, but laughter's divine,
In discomfort's garden, we create our own line.
With blooms that boast and thorns that jest,
We find joy in prickle; life's really the best!

Spiny Sentiments

In a world where spines make their debut,
A sunflower winked and batted a view.
She said, 'Dear friend, I feel slightly down,
But my leaves are still turning to greet the frown!'

A prickly pear squeaked, 'I'm quite charming, you know,
My spikes are just part of my glorious show!'
Roses chimed in, their smiles so sweet,
'Even our thorns can dance to the beat!'

With tangled emotions that rise and then dip,
A pun-filled unwinding, embrace in a trip.
Their laughter erupted, a raucous delight,
Planting joy in the soil, reaching new height.

In this garden of awkward, where sentiments bloom,
You'll find that a giggle can chase off the gloom.
So gather your blooms with spines that do sting,
And revel in chirps that every heart bring!

Ensnared by Reflection

In the mirror, I see a beast,
A monster with an unkempt feast.
My hair's a dance of chaos grand,
With socks that never seem to stand.

I ponder all the styles I've tried,
Each one a wave of joy applied.
Yet here I stand, a circus clown,
With mismatched shoes and nature's crown.

Every glance brings such a jest,
A laugh to welcome this strange quest.
With every wrinkle, grin, and smile,
I take life's chaos with a style.

So here's to mirrors, wild and free,
Reflecting whims, not always me.
In this dance of thoughts so rare,
I find the joy beyond compare.

Scattered Spines of Worry

My mind's a garden overgrown,
With worries sprouting all alone.
They tickle thoughts like prickly vines,
Producing laughter with their lines.

These spiky dreams jump here and there,
Like hedgehogs bouncing without care.
Each worry winds in loops and swirls,
As giggles clash with nature's pearls.

What if my plans all fall apart?
I'd merely lose a card or art.
They scatter fast like petals blown,
Yet in the chaos, joy is sown.

So let them sprout and twist about,
For scattered spines won't bring me doubt.
With every poke, I choose to grin,
And roll with quirks that hide within.

Clusters of Concern

Behold the clusters in my mind,
A jumble where the odd entwined.
They dance like squirrels in a fight,
In search of wisdom day and night.

Each little thought, a nut to share,
Caught here, there, in midair flair.
Yet giggles ring, their playful sound,
Make heavy worries spin around.

While clusters form and then dissolve,
Complexities that won't resolve.
I find it funny, this parade,
Of anxious thoughts that won't evade.

Embrace the chaos, let it roam,
For goofy quirks can find a home.
In every cluster born of strife,
I find the laughter in this life.

Riddles in the Understory

In the underbrush, a riddle lies,
With questions that elude the wise.
Why do socks mate, but never pair?
And why do ducks always seem to stare?

These thoughts like weeds entwine my brain,
They spark a giggle, entertain.
Each riddle wraps, then twists around,
Creating laughter from the ground.

What's lost beneath the couch of fate?
Those crumbs from snacks I should not rate?
With every question, joy takes flight,
As riddles bloom in morning light.

So here's to wonders, big and small,
That tickle us and make us fall.
In stories told, we find the glee,
And laugh at riddles set us free.

Twine of Turmoil

In the garden of my brain, plants arise,
They twist and tangle, oh what a surprise!
Trying to prune them feels like such a chore,
Yet they sprout new ideas—who could ask for more?

The daisies gossip, they chatter and sway,
While thorns mock me in a whimsical way.
Each thought is a vine, curling and steep,
A playful reminder before I sleep.

I tiptoe through dreams, with a laugh and a skip,
Each twist of my mind is a comic strip.
With humor in chaos, I dance through the night,
Embracing the mess, oh what a delight!

So here's to the knottiest, wildest spree,
Where even confusion can set the mind free.
In the twine of my thoughts, I take a bold stance,
For laughter, my friend, is the best kind of dance!

Snagged on Thought

Caught in a tangle, I trip on my wit,
Each thought like a sticker—oh, never quite fit.
I chuckle at concepts that snag on my brain,
Like socks in the dryer, they laugh at my pain.

A brilliant idea? It's lost in the mix,
Like trying to solve complex birdwatching tricks.
I laugh at the chaos, oh what a parade,
Thoughts darting around like a wild masquerade.

I reach for a notion, it zips past my hand,
Like a cat with a laser, it leads me to stand.
With every mishap, I grin a bit wider,
For even the mess can make joy seem brighter.

In the carnival of musings, I sit in the fray,
With giggles and snickers that come out to play.
Forgotten ideas? Just dust bunnies blown,
In the whirlwind of wonder, I'm never alone!

Bitter Realities

Life's little quirks are quite funny, I say,
Like stepping in gum on an otherwise fine day.
Each bitter truth wears a clown's painted grin,
As I slip on the truth, it's a slapstick win!

My dreams are like tacos, all messy and bright,
With toppings of worries, they wobble and bite.
I gulp down my pride with a sprinkle of fate,
Deliciously awkward—oh isn't it great?

Reality's nuggets can be quite absurd,
Like a hamster in glasses who thinks it's a bird.
With each misstep, I chuckle and roam,
Finding joy in confusion—that's how I feel home.

So here's to the wisdom locked up in jest,
To stumble through life is a most lively fest.
With bitterness melting in laughter's embrace,
I find every flaw is a ticklish grace!

Underneath the Petals

Beneath the blooms, where the laughter does grow,
Lies a riddle of thoughts wrapped in giggles and woe.
A bee with a wig buzzes by with flair,
While daisies gossip about who's wearing what hair.

Petals of wisdom drop light as a bubble,
Each color a story, each laugh hides some trouble.
With petals of pink and a daffodil grin,
I dance through the garden where silliness spins.

Oh, what fun to frolic in this floral mess,
With thoughts like confetti, a whimsical dress.
Where awkwardness twirls in a polka-dot tie,
And humor blooms brightly, reaching for the sky.

So let's dig through the leaves, let's giggle and play,
For underneath petals, there's magic at bay.
In a world full of whimsy, let joy be the guide,
With laughter our compass, there's nothing to hide!

Wounds of the Wandering Mind

My mind's a twisty maze, oh dear,
With ponderings that draw a sneer.
I tripped on thoughts, they snagged my shoe,
Now I'm lost in a thought stew.

I tried to think of simple things,
Like cats with wings and tiny rings.
But every time I seek some peace,
A new wild notion starts to tease.

Plans for lunch, then thoughts on cheese,
A parade of ideas that won't cease.
My brain's a circus with no end,
Where even clowns can't comprehend.

Oh mind of mine, so full of gunk,
You spin me 'round and leave me stunk.
Yet in this mess, I find my glee,
For laughter hides in every spree.

Veiled in Twisted Roots

In a garden of oddities, I find,
A web of roots that tangle the mind.
They whisper secrets, jumbled and sly,
Making me wonder, oh my, oh my!

"Is that a radish or my old shoe?"
I ask the plants for a little clue.
But they just giggle, a leafy jest,
While I'm left to ponder this strange quest.

I pruned my thoughts, yet they just sprout,
Each snip reveals a twisty route.
With each fresh leaf, I see the flaws,
As nature's humor jokes and claws.

Growing weeds of witticism tall,
I laugh at each confusing sprawl.
In the tangle, there's joy to seize,
For even roots can dance with ease.

Knots of Conundrum

Tangled up in my own head,
I trip on thoughts like tangled thread.
They knot and twist, a clever bind,
Leaving me puzzled, oh my mind!

Did I leave the stove on? Wait, what's new?
A sock's gone rogue, that can't be true!
I chase these antics, never on track,
As giggles pop from thoughts I lack.

Juggling ideas like they're fruit,
One goes splat! Oh what a hoot!
With every twist, I crack a smile,
For conundrums make life worthwhile.

So here I stand, a jester's pose,
With thoughts that wiggle and jiggle like prose.
In knots, I find my silly kind,
In the chaos, joy's entwined.

Grasping at Sharp Truths

I reached for truths, but they bite back,
Like poky plants in a sunny track.
Each answer sharp, a prickly tease,
Yet they make me chuckle, if you please.

"Is it true that ducks can wear hats?"
I ponder questions that baffle bats.
But those wise quackers just swim and laugh,
While I mull the math of a giraffe's path.

Truths can tickle or poke a bruise,
Yet searching brings laughter, no way to lose.
I grasp for logic, it slips away,
But joy fills the gaps in a curious way.

So here's to sharp things, full of jest,
In a world of wonders, I feel so blessed.
For the fun is in searching, no need to pout,
In this game of life, I'll never bail out.

The Thorned Serenade

In a garden filled with blooms,
I serenade the bees,
But guess who buzzed away fast?
My nose met with some leaves!

Petals fluttered, oh so bright,
While I pranced with flair,
But those prickly little stickers
Grew fond of my back hair!

With every step I take, alas,
There's a dance of pricks and stings,
They join my jolly jig tonight,
In a waltz of awkward flings!

Yet laughter fills the evening air,
As friends recount my plight,
Roses may be red, it's true,
But I'm the black-hatted knight!

Descent into the Thornbush

Adventuring on a sunny day,
Like a brave knight on his steed,
I stumbled into the thorny trap,
Thinking I was a bold breed!

I flailed and laughed at my own tricks,
As those spikes held me tight,
I swear I heard a cactus snicker,
While I wriggled left and right!

Oh, the birds above were chirping,
While I was stuck in place,
A floral comic ballet,
With thorns I couldn't face!

Friends laughed till they cried,
As I crafted my escape,
With my dignity in tatters bright,
But hey, I earned my cape!

Garlands of Grit

A crown of petals on my head,
Seemed like a grand idea,
But the thorns had other plans,
They whispered, "Oh, dear, oh dear!"

What a sight, my regal look,
With prickles poking proud,
I stood in front of my big mirror,
Feeling silly, oh so loud!

I posed for all my selfies bright,
But those thorns had quite the game,
"Transform your glam into a mess!"
They laughed and called my name!

I pranced around the kitchen floor,
With garlands made of grit,
Who knew that beauty came with laughs,
And a soft comedic hit!

Points of Pain

Here comes the dance with hot footed steps,
As I trounce through the garden's maze,
Each little prickle tells me, "Welcome!"
In this exciting game of phase!

With every leap, there's a tiny jab,
And I chuckle through the woe,
My feet may be sore, but my heart is light,
As I put on quite the show!

Friends gather 'round, they cheer and jeer,
At the antics of our afternoon,
With laughter ringing through the air,
As I dance a prickly tune!

So here's to all the little pokes,
That turn our laughs to rain,
In the merry mess we find our joy,
Amidst the little points of pain!

Shadows in the Garden of Doubt

In the garden where shadows creep,
I planted a smile, but it forgot to leap.
Roses whisper secrets, violets hide,
Yet somehow, I wear a cactus as my pride.

With petals of laughter, I danced in the breeze,
Every poke of a thorn brings me to my knees.
I chuckle at daisies, they giggle in glee,
While I'm tangled in brambles, wishing to flee.

The sun plays tricks, making weeds seem divine,
But every bright bloom hides a twist in the vine.
I sip on the nectar of thoughts gone astray,
And wonder if roses are here to stay.

So beware of the whispers, the giggles, the sighs,
For shadows will dance, and thorns will disguise.
With humor and irony stitched in my scarf,
I'll stroll through this garden, just trying to laugh.

The Briar's Embrace

In a corner of humor, the briar took hold,
It wrapped me in laughter, a sight to behold.
A tickle, a poke, with each step I take,
This prickly romance, I'm bound to awake.

With petals a-dancing, and stems holding sway,
I twirled with my anguish, come what may.
A chuckle erupted as I stumbled again,
The briar just winked, my mischievous friend.

It whispered sweet nothings, then pricked me with glee,
A soft, cheeky grin set the chaos free.
Each jab was a punchline, each throb just a jest,
In this cozy embrace, I found laughter's nest.

So here in this thicket, I'll cherish the jest,
Between prickles and giggles, I'm feeling quite blessed.
For life's full of thorns, but with humor I'm crowned,
In the briar's warm hug, true laughter is found.

Stingers of Solitude

In a room where the silence buzzed loud and deep,
I found a few stingers that made me peep.
Loneliness chuckled, with pins in its hand,
While I jested with shadows, my quirky band.

A laugh through the solitude, pricking my pride,
Every thought's a bee, wanting to hide.
Yet here I am buzzing, making a scene,
In a garden of giggles, where nobody's mean.

The hum of the worries, a comical tune,
Each thought takes flight, like a clumsy balloon.
With each little poke, I stretch and I bend,
Finding quirks in the quiet, my whimsical friend.

So I'll dance with the stingers, embrace every quirk,
Finding joy in the silence, a playful perk.
For solitude's laughter rings clear as a bell,
And in its sharp embrace, I'm doing quite well!

Choked by the Thicket

Lost in the thicket, where chirps meet the chirp,
I stumbled on laughter, then gave it a burp.
Rambunctious vines joked, tugging at my shirt,
While I rolled in the laughter, covered in dirt.

The foliage giggled, my shoes made a squish,
Tangling up antics, fulfilling my wish.
With every misstep, I grew roots around,
A plant in the comedy that whimsy had found.

Choked by the green, yet I'm grinning so wide,
Each twist of confusion fills laughter inside.
I swayed with the bushes that danced in delight,
Chasing shadows that hovered like stars in the night.

So here I am tangled, with joy in my heart,
In this jolly thicket, I've claimed my part.
Through laughter and pokes, I shall often roam,
For the thicket of giggles has made me a home.

The Searing Touch

When life's a joke, it pricks the skin,
Each laugh a spark, a wild grin.
Ticklish thoughts that dance around,
Like pogo sticks, they bounce and bound.

Hilarity hides in the sharpest puns,
A jester's fear, the pointy runs.
With every giggle, a prickly sting,
Oh, the joy that such thoughts bring!

From sunburned jokes to insults fleet,
Laughter's balm can't be beat.
Through laughter's maze, we take our chance,
Though sometimes we get pricked in the dance.

So here's to the fun, both sharp and bright,
In the prickly dance of joy and fright.
Embrace the jests that tease and knell,
For wispy laughter, we bid farewell.

In the Grip of Briars

Caught in laughter, sharp and sweet,
Briars of jest snagging my feet.
Twisting and turning through laughter's maze,
I giggle at my tangled ways.

A giggly waltz in a prickly dress,
I stumble, I tumble, oh what a mess!
With every jab a chuckle's born,
Among the thorns, I laugh 'til morn.

Tickle my ribs with witty schemes,
In prickle patches, we chase our dreams.
Friends gathered 'round, all bruised and sore,
But laughter's prizes are worth much more.

So let your thoughts run wild and free,
In this bramble patch, come join with me.
For every jab, there's joy indeed,
In the grip of briars, we plant the seed.

Barbs of Emotion

Emotions sharp, like cactus spines,
Tickling troubles, life's funny lines.
With every poke, a chuckle bursts,
Through all the pricks, we quench our thirsts.

A snarky comment here and there,
The barbs of humor, light as air.
Beneath the stings, the laughter flows,
In every jab, new joy bestows.

Each barb a little jab at fate,
We laugh and cry, but it's first-rate.
Emotion's dance, a prickly spree,
For in our hearts, we hold the key.

So poke some fun at life's grand scheme,
With each sharp jest, unleash the dream.
Let barbs of laughter freely roam,
In the garden of jest, we find our home.

A Bouquet of Barbs

Gather 'round for a floral jest,
A bouquet of barbs, it is the best.
Each petal a giggle, each thorn a tease,
In this garden of laughter, we find our ease.

With witty blooms and prickly cheer,
A cluster of fun, come lend your ear.
Watch out for the stems that tickle your side,
Among the laughs, we take our ride.

I smell the blooms of humor's grace,
In each sharp poke, we find our place.
A funny fest of rhymes and sprigs,
In laughter's arms, we feel the jigs.

So share this bouquet, don't let it wilt,
For every barb is joy we built.
With laughter's bloom, we mend the rift,
In a world of barbs, we share the gift.

Scourge of Serenity

In the garden of my mind, weeds grow,
Thoughts like little ninjas, they steal the show.
Jokes sprout up in chaos, all askew,
I chuckle at the madness, a wacky view.

A dandelion dressed in a suit and tie,
Bargains with the butterflies flying high.
Laughter erupts as I trip on a vine,
Nature's own prankster, oh how divine!

Roses giggle as their petals fall,
While bees perform dances, having a ball.
My head spins with visions of pure delight,
To the soundtrack of nature, my mind takes flight.

But as I sip tea, all calm and bright,
A gopher appears, it gives me a fright.
Serenity's scourge, a comic display,
In this whimsical garden, I find my way.

A Thorn in the Mind

A prickly thought sneaks up, oh dear,
Like a cat in a hat with nothing to fear.
It bounces around, causing such fuss,
Who knew that thoughts could be so nonplussed?

A cactus stares down, it rolls its eyes,
As I try to reason, with no goodbyes.
My brain is a pinball, it ricochets bright,
Every thought a little imp, dancing in flight.

I offer my mind a comfy retreat,
But the thorns laugh as they shuffle their feet.
They conspire and plot, a comical gang,
My mental circus in a tangled twang!

Yet in the chaos, I find a sweet glee,
These thorny antics bring laughter to me.
Though poked and prodded, I can't help but smile,
In this whimsical maze, I'll linger awhile.

Prickled Perceptions

My thoughts wobble like jelly on a plate,
One rolls away, oh what a fate!
A pickle parade through my tangled head,
Each merely a jest, no need to dread.

Beneath the surface, thorns lurk like jesters,
They poke and they prowl, mischief investors.
A jolly old gnome tickles my brain,
With riddles and puns, I dance in the rain.

Silly notions tied up in knots,
Like socks in the dryer, forgetting their pots.
I giggle at antics, ridiculous sights,
A circus of ideas, on whimsical flights.

Yet as I tumble through this zany maze,
I find joy nestled in the thorny haze.
Prickled perceptions weave stories anew,
Each laugh a reminder, life's joy is true!

The Pain Within

A tickle, a poke, a nag in my head,
Thoughts play hopscotch, but some are misled.
I've got a circus, a funny little show,
Where thoughts shimmy and shake, just go with the flow.

The pain within feels like a pie in the face,
Each thought is a slice, of a giggly disgrace.
I roll on the floor, laughter a balm,
As silly ideas weave chaos, yet calm.

But just when I think that all is quite fine,
A cactus in slippers sits down to dine.
It feasts on my worries with glee in its eyes,
While I chortle at the absurdness that flies.

With every poke comes a chuckle or two,
Life's funny little thorns grow on me and you.
So let's dance through the stings, with laughter and grace,
In the wacky wild garden, let joy find its space!

The Painful Bloom

In a garden of giggles, I trip and I fall,
With daisies that surely have a mind of their own.
They whisper sweet nothings, then give me a call,
And poke me with laughter, I'm honed to be shown.

The roses are radiant, yet fierce in their play,
They dance in the sun, then I dodge their sharp quips.
Each petal a punchline, in colorful array,
A bouquet of banter that teases and slips.

The tulips are tricky, with jokes up their sleeves,
They giggle as I wander, so lost in their maze.
I ponder my fortune, the thorns make me grieve,
Yet chuckles keep bursting; I'm wrapped in their gaze.

In this field of folly, I chuckle and muse,
Who knew that the blossoms could truly be bold?
Each giggle a thorn, yet I can't help but choose,
To frolic with flowers that shimmer like gold.

Tangled Mindscapes

In the tangle of thoughts where the wild weeds grow,
I stumble and shuffle, but laughter's my mate.
Each twist is a tickle; oh where will I go?
I'm lost in the maze, but I savor the fate.

My brain's like a garden, with thoughts all askew,
Some flowers are daisies, others pointy vines.
I laugh at my musings, surreal but so true,
In this mental jungle, I'm throwing out lines.

The bees are a chatter, like buzzing for fun,
They zigzag my thoughts, each buzz is a wink.
Plucking petals of chaos, I laugh and I run,
Ignoring the thorns as I dance on the brink.

Tangled and twisted, this lattice of glee,
Each layer a giggle, each branch brings a smile.
In the clutches of madness, I'm still feeling free,
Here's to tangled mindscapes that tickle my style.

Spines of the Soul

In the depths of my being, there's prickles that tease,
A feeling of foibles that sometimes emerge.
With spines of my soul, I giggle with ease,
Each jab is a jest, like life's little dirge.

The laughter it echoes, a whimsical sound,
As thorns poke and prod, yet they're soft to the touch.
I find joy in the jests that are scattered around,
Every sharp little quip is amusing too much.

Their wisdom they share in a cheeky parade,
With every sly poke, there's a chuckle to glean.
These spines are like laughter, in sunshine or shade,
Each jab is inviting, though sometimes obscene.

So here's to the prickers, the jesters at play,
They tickle my spirit, igniting my soul.
With spines that may sting, turn my frown into play,
I'll dance with their jibes, in this rollicking scroll.

Bitter Petals

The petals may bitterly bruise and they clash,
Their laughter so sharp makes me shake and I grin.
A zany concoction of flowers that splash,
Their giggles are salty, I dive in with spin.

These buds tease my dreams with a playful embrace,
Oh, the irony dances on each flowery head.
While smiles set the stage for a comical race,
Glimmers of giggles bloom bright where I tread.

But underneath colors, there's wisdom so coy,
For laughter can gallop on paths that are rough.
In bitterness hiding is heartwarming joy,
Each petal, a riddle that's silly enough.

So here's to the garden where laughter's the rule,
I'll roam through the flowers and relish the view.
With bitter and funny, I'll fashion a jewel,
In a world where the petals are joyfully blue.

The Sorrowful Thorn

In a garden full of blooms, joy reigns,
But here I am, and it still pains.
Petals whisper soft and sweet,
Yet my heart just cannot beat.

A prickly crown upon my head,
Does it mean I'm unwell, or just misled?
I try to smile, but it's quite tough,
With every step, I'm just a puff.

Friends say I'm unique, full of flair,
But I'm just sharp and in despair.
Like hedgehogs wearing hats too tight,
I giggle on, yet cradle my plight.

So I seek a patch of light and fun,
Where thorns are friends, and we all run.
I'll dance with blooms—what a sight to see,
As I dodge their jabs, just let me be!

Paradox of the Bloom

In this flowerbed, I stand alone,
Dancing with thorns, yet I'm so prone.
Blooming brightly, all eyes on me,
Yet I poke a hole in your glee.

With petals like whispers, light as air,
I reach for laughs, but beware the snare.
A prick, a giggle, a twist of fate,
Is it a flower or just a mate?

I wear the smile of bright delight,
But it's my poky parts that steal the light.
Laughing loudly is an art, they say,
Just try not to trip on the thorny way!

Life's a riddle wrapped in a jest,
With every bloom, I feel more stressed.
But laughter's the key to ease the pain,
Join me, dear friend, it's less of a strain!

The Cacophony of Thorns

In a garden where the chaos rings,
The thorns chuckle, oh, the joy it brings.
They flap about, so loud and brash,
And I, the fool, just crash and clash.

What's that they say? Just stand up tall,
But with prickers about, I doubt my call.
Flailing, flinging, why's this a sport?
Each jab just feels like a quirky retort.

We meet and greet with prickly cheer,
Who knew that pain could feel so dear?
Through fits of laughter, our banter flows,
In the mix of thorns, delight still grows.

So here I wade, in a jolly mess,
With brambles and giggles, I must confess.
A cacophony blooms with each little sting,
As I embrace the song that only thorns bring!

Just a Sting Away

Laughter hides behind a spiky mask,
A tickle here, a poke—what a task!
Just a sting away from bursting free,
   Yet here I sit, sharp as can be.

Friends gather 'round to share their woes,
   But I just poke, as humor grows.
   In jokes we find a sharp delight,
As we dance with thorns into the night.

Just when you think it's all a blur,
I'll get you close for a friendly spur.
Giggles erupt like bubbles in air,
As I'm snorting while they pull their hair.

So let's toast to fun that prickles the heart,
With laughter leading, we'll never part.
Just a sting away, let's laugh all day,
In a garden of humor, let's play, let's play!

Thorns Beneath Skin

Brought my cactus to the beach,
Sunburnt spines, they seem to preach.
Laughter dances in the air,
Prickly jokes, a funny affair.

My friend slips on the sandy ground,
Yells, "Look out! A spiky mound!"
We all burst into chuckling fits,
As prickly woes become our wits.

In the garden, blooms are bright,
But watch your step, they're full of bite.
A poke here and a jab right there,
"And I thought flowers were so rare!"

The comedy of gardening's plight,
With every thump and clumsy fight.
Who knew nature could be this bold?
In a world of thorns, hilarity unfolds!

Barbed Wire Dreams

In my dreams, I climb so high,
But tangled wire makes me sigh.
I reach for stars, they slip away,
Laughing echoes, "What a display!"

A hedgehog smiles, as I get stuck,
"Don't take it hard, just laugh and duck!"
Bouncing back from each harsh snag,
"Life's a circus," I slyly brag.

Fashion shows of fancied furs,
I prance in dreams just like a blur.
But watch out for those pesky pricks,
My runway's fate—complete with kicks!

In the land of giggles and ropes,
Barbed wire dreams, full of hopes.
We chuckle as we face each fence,
Finding humor in the suspense!

Jarring Realities

Woke up to the clatter of pots,
Realities hit like unwanted thoughts.
"Oops!" I squeal, as I trip and fall,
Laughter echoes, my wake-up call.

In the kitchen, chaos reigned,
With every dish a loss attained.
I laughed at burned and charred cuisine,
"Who knew cooking could be so mean?"

A doorbell ring—what a surprise!
Cactus mailman in disguise!
"Sign here, please," he tugs my sleeve,
"With spiky joy, you'll not believe!"

Jarring truths and goofy sights,
Life's a mix of fun-filled fights.
We weave our tales, with laughs we sew,
Through prickled paths, our spirits grow!

Twisting Paths of Reflection

In the mirror, my face distorts,
Twisting paths of quirk and retorts.
I see a crown of twigs and leaves,
"Haha! Nature's what deceives!"

Each bend unveils a funny side,
As I giggle, my cheeks grow wide.
Reflections dance with jibes and jests,
Finding laughter is what's best.

With every poke and every jab,
I navigate this thorny slab.
But with a grin and winks to share,
"Life's a ride, so grab a chair!"

In twisty thoughts where humor's found,
We celebrate the silly sound.
Through barbs and jests, we pave our way,
In mirthful paths, we choose to stay!

The Unspoken Prick

In a garden of giggles, I tripped on a bee,
Whispering secrets, said, "Stay away from me!"
A clumsy ballet in a sunny parade,
I wore pollen like confetti, was feeling quite played.

With a hat made of thistles, I danced with a grin,
Twisting my way through the prickly, the thin.
Each poke was a chuckle, each scratch was a laugh,
Nature's own way of showing the path.

While my thoughts were all tangled, I laughed at the sting,
A playful reminder of the joy that they bring.
So I waltzed with my worries, a hysterical show,
In the garden of life, what a curious flow!

In the realm of the restless, I found a small cheer,
Where each little prickles giggles, never fear!
I'll write 'em a letter and send it a-fly,
To the thorns that bring laughter, oh, how they can pry!

Rooted Turmoil

Digging deep in my mind, there's a tangle of glee,
With roots wrapped around, not quite sure what I see.
Thoughts sprout like daisies, a bloom of mishaps,
Entwined in the laughter, I'm lost in the traps.

Each twist and each turn, a comedic delight,
Stumbling through moments that keep me up at night.
Who knew that confusion could tickle so much?
I laugh at the chaos, it's love in its touch.

Oh, the roots of my worry twist tight like a vine,
But I wriggle and giggle, proclaiming it's fine.
In this forest of folly, I sway with the breeze,
Embracing the silliness that tickles with ease.

So here's to the muddle, the mess and the fuss,
Where tangled thoughts frolic and cause quite the ruckus,
With each little hiccup, I wear the crown bold,
In this comedy garden, my heart turns to gold!

Entangled Reflections

A mirror of mayhem, I'm tangled in fun,
Reflecting on moments, all wacky, not one.
My brain's like a puzzle, with pieces that shout,
Each wobbly thought on a humorous route.

I stumbled on laughter, it caught me off guard,
With clarity hidden, and my vision a shard.
Fuzzy logic giggles, like a cat chasing tails,
In the labyrinth of nonsense, creativity sails.

Amidst all the chaos, there's charm to be found,
With whispers of whimsy that echo around.
Undone by the tickles of thoughts that entwine,
In a tangled reflection, I find that I shine.

So here's to the daftness, the grace in the mess,
With each little hiccup, I simply confess,
These quirky entanglements pull on my heart,
In this dance of absurdity, I play my part!

Invasive Introspection

Invasive ideas make camp in my head,
Like weeds in my garden, they flourish instead.
With a giggle and snicker, I battle the day,
Poking at ponderings in funny array.

I prance through my thoughts like a bunny gone wild,
Each tumble and hiccup keeps me like a child.
Reflecting on nonsense like it's some grand theme,
Being silly and playful, a whimsical dream.

Oh, the joy in the chaos, a riddle, a jest,
Where logic gets tangled, and nonsense feels best.
Invasive introspection, a clown at the core,
Tickling my fancy, always wanting more.

So let's dance with the madness, let's twirl with the spin,
Lift the curtain of calm, let the chuckling begin.
With laughter as armor, I claim it with delight,
In this wacky existence, everything feels right!

Tangles of the Unsung

In the garden where I roam,
My brain's a tangle like a gnome.
Thoughts like weeds, they twist and creep,
In laughter's light, I lose my sleep.

A chicken thought, it crossed my mind,
What if it laid eggs left behind?
With every giggle, worries fade,
I ponder on the choices made.

Jumbled dreams of socks in pairs,
Of dancing goats and wild hares.
In this chaos, I find my cheer,
Each silly thought, I hold them dear.

And so, I skip with joy unbound,
In the mess, sweet laughter's found.
Embrace the twists, the smiles and grins,
For life's a dance, where fun begins.

The Edge of Bramble

On the edge of a prickly scene,
Where thoughts are wild, though not too mean.
I trip on wishes, tumble through,
In this bramble, I find my crew.

An idea sprouted, all ablaze,
It's set to dance, in silly ways.
What if hiccups wrote a book?
With every laugh, the world we took.

I chase my dreams like buzzing flies,
Through buzzing thoughts and goofy sighs.
With every bump, a story sways,
In laughter's lap, my heart delays.

So join me here, in funny plight,
Where worries vanish, out of sight.
At this bramble's charming edge,
We'll dance and laugh, and still allege.

Unraveled in the Underbrush

In underbrush where giggles play,
My thoughts unwind like yarn, hooray!
A twist of fate, a joke unfolds,
In tangled lines, rich laughter molds.

What if my socks were made of cheese?
And mice came by to take their ease?
In this forest of silly schemes,
I weave my heart into my dreams.

Beneath the leaves, absurdity blooms,
With talking plants and singing brooms.
Here in the chaos, joy is found,
In every chuckle, life astounds.

So let's get lost, come take the ride,
Through silly paths where fun is wide.
In underbrush, we'll laugh until,
Unraveled, we embrace the thrill.

Searing Dilemmas

My mind's a grill with thoughts on high,
Searing questions that make me sigh.
Like toast on fire, I ponder long,
Amidst the smoke, I hum a song.

What to choose for lunch today,
A pickle pie or fish ballet?
With each decision, giggles grow,
As silly forks and spoons bestow.

I juggle options like a clown,
While thoughts conspire to bring me down.
But in the heat, I find my groove,
Embracing quirks, I start to move.

So here I stand, in funny plight,
Flipping dilemmas with pure delight.
With laughter sharp, my path is clear,
In searing chaos, joy is near.

Petals Amidst the Thorns

Amidst the roses, I fail to see,
Why I can't find a bumblebee.
They're buzzing along, so full of cheer,
While I'm just here, sipping my beer.

The petals are soft, but what's this I found?
A prickly surprise, waiting around!
With laughter I dance, as I wobble and sway,
Finding humor in thorns that won't go away.

The garden's a joke, I chuckle with glee,
Each bloom has its bark, most certainly!
But aren't we all just a little absurd,
Wrestling with prickles and dreams unheard?

So gather the petals, ignore the sting,
Life's full of giggles, let laughter bring.
With thorns on the side, let's twirl and spin,
We'll make a bouquet of the chaos within!

Hooked by Hesitation

One thought leads me down a merry lane,
But here comes a prickle to drive me insane!
Should I take that leap, or stay on the line?
The choice is a dance, a riddle divine.

I tiptoe through options, a delicate tease,
Each step feels like fun, yet lacking the ease.
Should I dive in, or just sip my drink?
Oh, why does it matter? I'm here to think!

The hook of indecision pulls me so tight,
Like a sock in the dryer, lost out of sight.
While I ponder the jumps, I crack up alone,
How life is a circus, with thoughts on loan.

So I'll chuckle and wobble, embrace the unknown,
With a wink at the thorns I've utterly sown.
For laughter's the key, or so they all say,
Letting go of my doubts, I'm ready to play!

The Snare of Thought

In the webs of my mind, I tangle and twist,
Thoughts turn to thorns that simply insist.
I hop like a rabbit, then freeze in a glare,
Why's pondering life like picking a hair?

Each giggle appears, yet the giggles mislead,
Tangled in riddles, I'm swallowed in greed.
The punchline is hidden, I'm catching my breath,
In a forest of nonsense, I'm playing with death.

So I dance 'round the logic, all snippy and spry,
As thoughts sneak behind me, I laugh and I cry.
Like a cat with a cucumber, I'm startled and whole,
Life's just a puzzle with holes, that's the goal!

I'll untangle my whims, with a smile and a cheer,
For laughter's the snare that keeps bringing me near.
Amidst all the madness, I'll twirl and I'll twine,
Finding joy in the chaos, and all will be fine!

Splintered Wishes

Oh, wishing on stars can lead to sharp ends,
With hopes that are splintered, they twist like my friends.
I toss out a wish, it squeaks and it squeals,
What happened to magic? It vanished with meals!

Like a kite in a tree, I swing high and low,
Each wish is a puzzle that simply won't flow.
I'll laugh at the splinters, embrace the odd feels,
Finding joy in the whims that life oft reveals.

So I gather my wishes, both silly and small,
And tie them together, in one big ball.
With a wink and a nudge, I'll let them all fly,
While chuckling at life as it whirls by and by!

For wishes may splinter, but humor will bloom,
In the garden of jest, I'll chase off the gloom.
So here's to the laughter, the fun, and the cheer,
I'll wish for good vibes for another whole year!

Grit and Grace

In the garden of grumpy blooms,
Petals dance with gloomy tunes.
They poke and prod, oh what a fate,
Yet here we laugh, we procrastinate.

With every prick, a chuckle shared,
A poke of humor, none are scared.
Life's jabs may come, round and round,
But who knew laughs could be so profound?

In this wilderness, we find our way,
Dodging barbs that seem to stay.
We twirl and dip like dandy fools,
Finding joy in our own laughable tools.

The Cutting Edge

Oh, the edges done so sharp,
Like dogs that howl and cats that harp.
Funny how the world can sting,
With every jab, we dance and swing.

Here comes a shard that tries to bite,
But we just giggle, what a sight!
Like clowns on stilts, precarious and wild,
We juggle life, the joke's compiled.

With every snip, a little glee,
A punchline waiting, can't you see?
We dodge and weave, our spirits high,
As pointed pranks fly by, oh my!

Shadows in the Garden

In the shadows where laughter waits,
We stumble on our silly fates.
Behind the flowers, whispers play,
Ticklish giggles, come what may.

Beneath the leaves, a ticklish breeze,
Oh, the antics—such a tease!
We skip through thorns like crazed ballet,
Forget the ouches, hip-hip-hurray!

With shadows lurking, we trip and fall,
Yet with each tumble, we own it all.
The garden giggles at our plight,
Under the moon, everything feels right.

Porcupine Thoughts

Woke up with pricks in my brain,
Like porcupines on a crowded train.
Thoughts are wild, they dance and dart,
A ticklish maze with a cheeky heart.

Shuffling ideas that poke and prod,
Each one a giggle, oh how they applaud!
In the spiky chaos, laughter stays,
For it's the quirks that brighten our days.

Whimsical pricks, they bring such cheer,
Funny little thoughts that linger near.
So let them prickle, let them shine,
For every poke reveals the divine.

Untamed Reflections

In the garden of my brain, a jest,
Ideas sprout, then fail the test.
With every thought that tries to shine,
A chuckle blooms, so sweet, divine.

Wrinkles of laughter, twisty turns,
Catchy quips, my brain just yearns.
I trip on jokes, they scratch my mind,
But oh, the fun! It's one of a kind.

Puns are jumping, dancing free,
My inner clown just threw a spree.
A self-proclaimed circus of silly men,
Clowns with wisdom—a paradox then.

So here I sit, with thoughts astray,
Spiky giggles rule my day.
I'll gather laughs, both wild and tame,
In this madcap circus, I'm to blame.

Restless Briars

Beneath the laughs, a prickly dream,
My mind's a garden, bursting at the seam.
Rambunctious ideas clash and play,
As punchlines wiggle, leading me astray.

Fluffy thoughts atop the thorns,
Witty riddles live and mourn.
Cacti giggle in the afternoon sun,
Nature's jests, oh what fun!

Twisted tales, a quirky plot,
Every brainstorm's like a shot.
Yet here I drown in laughter's bliss,
Finding joy in a spiky kiss.

So let them dance, these restless minds,
In tangled paths, adventure finds.
A prick here, a poke there,
Amongst the fun, I shed my care.

The Silent Prick

In quiet corners of my head,
Whispers tickle, break the thread.
A subtle jab, a muted jest,
Brings out the giggles, I must confess.

Thoughts like daisies, but sharp with glee,
I laugh at shadows—who's prickly?
Each fun-filled ponder, a raucous shout,
Where silliness casts shadows out.

I stroll through paths where chuckles cling,
A silent jab, but oh, it sings!
With every poke, the humor grows,
Planting joy, just see how it glows.

So tiptoe lightly in this spree,
Where pricks of laughter set us free.
Join this dance of quips and laughs,
In this bliss, forget the paths.

Echoes of a Thorn

Echoes bounce in my crowded mind,
Thoughts ricochet, but aren't unkind.
Hilarity's dance, a twist and shout,
With every jab, we laugh it out.

In quiet corners, mischief reigns,
A prickly poke, it entertains.
Gags and giggles bloom like flowers,
Sprouting jokes in unexpected hours.

Amid the jangle of wild ideas,
There's a universe of chuckling cheers.
Each snicker blooms, a cheeky thorn,
Blossoming born from the absurd and worn.

So let the echoes play their tune,
While I giggle underneath the moon.
With prickly joy, I take the plunge,
In this garden of mirth, let's all expunge.

Woe's Embrace

In my garden of woes, I plant a laugh,
A cackle sprout, like a green giraffe.
Worries wander, tripping on roots,
With every tumble, they whistle in suits.

Butterflies gossip, tickled by glee,
While crickets play poker, sipping iced tea.
I chase my thoughts, like a playful kite,
They loop and dive, oh what a sight!

Amidst the thorns, a rainbow appears,
Tickling my frown and tickling my tears.
I'll dance with the weeds in this playful spree,
With every step, happy chaos is free!

So let blooms of giggles in silence erupt,
As daisies poke fun, oh, how they disrupt!
In this crazy garden where my mind does race,
I'll wear my laughter like a bright bouquet lace.

Hidden Thickets

In a forest of thoughts, I lost my way,
A squirrel with glasses guiding my play.
He chuckles and chatters, holding a map,
While I trip on a twig, landing with a slap.

Branches are bending, whispers are loud,
A fox in a cloak is under a shroud.
"Follow the giggles!" he shouts quite a lot,
And I tumble through bushes, hoping to plot.

Amid slippery slopes of ideas that cling,
I find laughter hidden—a mischievous spring.
With each step I take, the brambles twist tight,
But they can't stop the chuckles that burst into flight!

So here in these thickets, I'll dance, twirl, and play,
Chasing the echoes of laughter all day.
In a tangle of thorns, there's joy to explore,
For sometimes the laughter's the best part of lore.

Fragmented Fronds

Leaves of worry flutter, a chaotic display,
With giggles entwined in a curious way.
I gather the fragments, the bits and the pieces,
Creating a crown where silliness increases.

Petals confide in the shadows they caught,
Whispering secrets that meaning forgot.
I chuckle and pout, a parade in my mind,
As I chase down the fragments, so childlike and blind.

While daisies keep blushing, the roses just grin,
With pollen confetti, let the party begin!
In the garden of fumbles, we make such a scene,
Waving to laughter like overgrown green.

So here I sit, sipping sunshine from vines,
As irony dances in winding designs.
With each fragmented thought, I paint with delight,
Composing a canvas that shines through the night.

Gritted Roots

Underneath the surface, where giggles reside,
Gritty roots chuckle, they never do hide.
They tickle my toes as I wander around,
In a labyrinth of laughter where joy can be found.

The dirt plays a tune, with a whimsical tune,
While worms with top hats hold a gala at noon.
The thunderous chuckles shake dirt from my shoe,
Embracing the chaos, come join the hullabaloo!

These roots weave stories of silly and spry,
Entwined in the mischief, oh, how they fly!
With every step forward, a giggle erupts,
As secrets of laughter bubble up and disrupt.

So let's stomp through this soil where whimsy does bloom,
In the laughter of roots, life's the best kind of zoom.
With gritted attention to fun at the core,
I'll dance with the roots, eternally more!

The Twine of Woes

In a garden of giggles, I tripped on my fate,
Roses whisper secrets, but I'm always late.
A tangle of vines, oh what a delight,
With every step forward, I'm stuck in mid-flight.

The daisies are laughing, I hear their loud cheer,
But my shoelace is tied to a bush, oh dear!
I tumble and tumble, a slapstick display,
With thorns on my jeans, I hilariously sway.

The sun beams a grin, I can't help but chuckle,
While nettles around me begin to snuggle.
I've learned life's a dance, a precarious jig,
And sometimes the best part is just being big.

So here's to the moments of awkward despair,
When laughter surrounds us and floats in the air.
I'll embrace all the blunders, they add to the fun,
For life is a circus, and I'm just a pun!

Pensive Prickers

A poke in the side, it tickles a thought,
Why do cacti wear crowns, are they all just distraught?
I ponder the prickles, all sharp yet so sly,
While wondering if they just want to fly.

With whimsies of humor, the thorns start to jest,
As I laugh at my worries, they crumble like zest.
I wrestle with giggles, their sharpness so grand,
My mind's like a playground, all wild and unplanned.

A garden of whimsy, where sighs turn to cheer,
Like pickles in brine, our thoughts disappear.
I slip on the banter, a smooth comic glide,
Through prickers of laughter, I'm joyfully tied.

So smile at the jabs, they're all in good fun,
Let humor be gentle, it's how we have won.
With each step I take, I embrace every tease,
For life's just a laughter, and thorns are the squeeze!

Splinters of Truth

In the forest of ponder, where thoughts like wood grow,
I've tripped on a splinter of wisdom, oh no!
Each piece that I gather, it tickles my mind,
With jests in the shadows, I'm humorously blind.

The trees chuckle softly, their branches all sway,
As I dance 'round the stumps, in a clumsy ballet.
With splinters that sparkle, like laughter in air,
I giggle with nature, oh what a fair!

The leaves whisper secrets, all sharp and absurd,
While I write down my fables, a jester's unheard.
Each truth I uncover is pricked by a laugh,
In a maze of confusion, I'm taking a bath!

So here's to the splinters that poke and rejoice,
In the heart of my thoughts, they make a loud noise.
With every odd moment, I'll cherish the fun,
For laughter's the light, and we're never outdone!

Hedged Emotions

Between the hedges, my feelings take flight,
While chuckling at roses that bloom in the night.
A hedge trimmed for laughter, with clippers in tow,
I snip at my worries, they laugh as they go.

Like squirrels in topsy-turvy dance on a branch,
I giggle through shadows, a figment, a chance.
With emotions like brambles, they tug at my heart,
But I'm leaping and skipping, a whimsical art.

The flowers are gossiping, wrapped in their show,
While my thoughts trip on petals, they twist and they flow.
I dive into humor, face first in a bush,
With thorns on my cheeks, I emerge with a hush.

So here's to the hedges, they keep me alive,
With snippets of joy, I find ways to thrive.
In every sharp moment, a poke from the past,
I'll giggle and dance, till the very last blast!

www.ingramcontent.com/pod-product-compliance
Lightning Source LLC
Chambersburg PA
CBHW070751220426
43209CB00083B/818